The Crisis of Democracy

Weixiong Li

DEDICATION

To my parents and my wife, Cindy.

CONTENTS

PREFACE

When I left my job as a hedge-fund analyst in the summer of 2007 to become an independent investor, little did I know that the world economic and financial landscape was at the cusp of a tectonic shift. The turbulence I had witnessed during the financial crisis from late 2007 through early 2009 and the ensuing political and economic aftershocks that have played out (and are still developing today) in America and Europe led me to thoroughly reexamine the very foundation on which the developed world has been built over the last several centuries. The result is this little book.

Although democracy is the best political system humanity has ever invented, it is by no means infallible. In reality, democracy is fragile and prone to abuse. It requires constant care and nurturing from citizens in order to survive and thrive. This book analyzes several fundamental flaws that democratic societies share, and it demonstrates how these flaws, after decades of neglect and abuse, inevitably lead to social difficulties that much of the developed world is experiencing today.

In laying out my thesis, I have tried to be objective and nonpartisan. Too often, I have seen debates in which participants start with political ideologies that are already deeply rooted in their minds; they then look for superficial correlations to support their respective political views. For example, conservatives often justify their tax-cut policies by citing the success of the Reagan era, while liberals frequently argue in favor of raising taxes because of the strong economic growth during the Clinton administration. In reality, the effects of these different tax policies had more to do with the different prevailing tax rates and economic conditions at their respective times. At a prohibitively high top tax rate of 70 percent, a Reagan tax cut proved effective, but at an already low top rate of 28 percent, an increase in tax rate brought us more benefits, such as reducing income inequality and national debt. Indeed, the prosperity America enjoyed in the 1980s and 1990s likely had more to do with the earlier bold moves by former Federal Reserve Chairman Paul Volcker, the subsequent secular upswing of the economic cycle, and the invention of the Internet than with the economic policies of either political party. Partisan debates like these are common in our national politics today, but they add very little value in the effort to improve our society. Therefore, throughout this book, rather than allowing myself to be influenced by partisan bias, I have made every effort to develop my thesis by objective reasoning and logic.

i

I make frequent references to Wikipedia throughout this book. I have also benefited from the work of Professor Nassim Taleb by reading his publications and watching his publically available speeches. Although largely shunned by mainstream economics professionals today, I believe history will eventually prove many of his views and warnings to be prescient. The only questions are how long it will take for society to recognize this and what price society will have paid for the flawed policies that are so prevalent today.

1 THE POLITICAL AND ECONOMIC SYSTEMS OF SOCIETY

A Two-Dimensional Characterization of Nations

Two dimensions characterize modern societies. The first dimension is the economic system, whether it is capitalism or socialism. The second dimension is the political system, whether it is a democracy or an autocracy. Any nation can be represented by a point on such a two-dimensional diagram, as shown in figure 1.

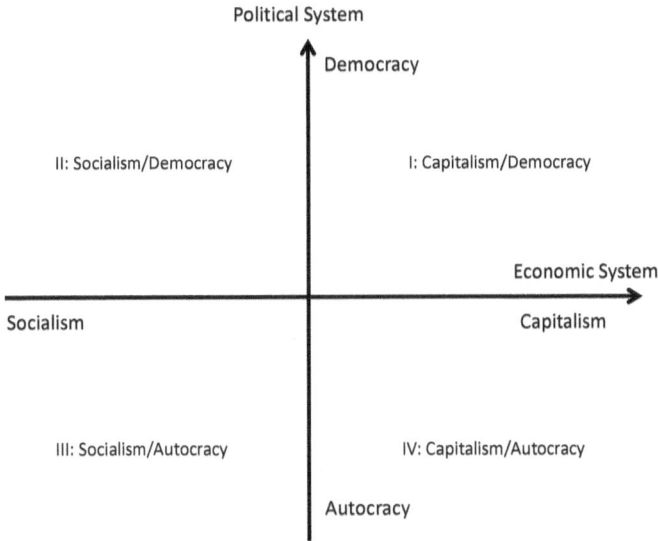

Figure 1 Economic/Political System

There are, therefore, four possible types of nations in the world:
- Type 1: nations with capitalism and democracy (first quadrant)
- Type 2: nations with socialism and democracy (second quadrant)
- Type 3: nations with socialism and autocracy (third quadrant)
- Type 4: nations with capitalism and autocracy (fourth quadrant)

Capitalism versus Socialism

According to Wikipedia, "Capitalism is an economic system based on private ownership of the means of production and their operation for profit."[1]

---

[1] "Capitalism," Wikipedia, November 11, 2016,
https://en.wikipedia.org/wiki/Capitalism

On the other hand, "Socialism is an economic system based on the social ownership and control of the means of production; as well as a political and economic theory, ideology and movement that aims at the establishment of a socialist system."[2]

Therefore, the fundamental difference between capitalism and socialism lies in the different ownership structure and motivation of businesses. It should be emphasized that in the real world, pure capitalism or socialism is rare, if not impossible. For example, China, while still largely a socialist country, has a very vibrant and expanding private-sector economy. The United States, on the other hand, has seen its more pure form of capitalism gradually eroding since the Great Depression. This happened as the government played more and more prominent roles in the nation's economy, ranging from social-welfare policy to fiscal policy to monetary policy. Therefore, most countries lie in between pure forms of capitalism and socialism, depending on the relative weight between the private-sector and public-sector economies.

Democracy versus Autocracy

According to Wikipedia, democracy "is a system of government in which the citizens exercise power directly or elect representatives from among themselves to form a governing body"[3].

On the other hand, "An autocracy is a system of government in which supreme power is concentrated in the hands of one person, whose decisions are subject to neither external legal restraints nor regularized mechanisms of popular control."[4]

Therefore, the fundamental difference between democracy and autocracy lies in the collective power of the people. In a democracy, people can change the government and have the ultimate power. In an autocracy, people are mostly powerless, and the only way to change government is through a coup or popular revolution.

Nations sometimes adopt mixed forms of government. One such example is China. While not yet a democratic society, China has evolved

---

[2] "Socialism (disambiguation)," Wikipedia, November 11, 2016, https://en.wikipedia.org/wiki/Socialism_(disambiguation)

[3] "Democracy," Wikipedia, November 11, 2016, https://en.wikipedia.org/wiki/Democracy

[4] "Autocracy," Wikipedia, November 11, 2016, https://en.wikipedia.org/wiki/Autocracy

from Mao's era of autocracy to the current form of collective leadership, which differs from Mao's autocracy in two ways: first, there is a committee (the politburo) that constrains the power of the president, and second, the presidency has a term limit (ten years).

Global Geopolitical Trends

If we examine nations through this two-dimensional view of their political-economic systems, we notice some interesting patterns. (See figure 2.) For example, since the end of World War II, most Western countries have adopted both capitalism and democracy. Developing countries, on the other hand, have mostly adopted socialism with almost no democracy. This pattern, however, has changed significantly since the end of the Cold War. One of the most successful stories in world geopolitics over the last fifty years has been the amazing transitions of Asian tiger countries, such as South Korea and Singapore, from autocratic societies into capitalistic democracies. Such transformation, largely under American influence and leadership, has not only benefited the people in the region but also provided examples of reform for other countries such as China. As a result, socialist countries in the developing world began to allow more private-sector economies to augment their state-controlled economies, and with that, political systems in these counties became more relaxed. On the other hand, European countries, and more recently the United States, while still highly democratic, have become more socialistic as a result of their quests for more social welfare and benefits.

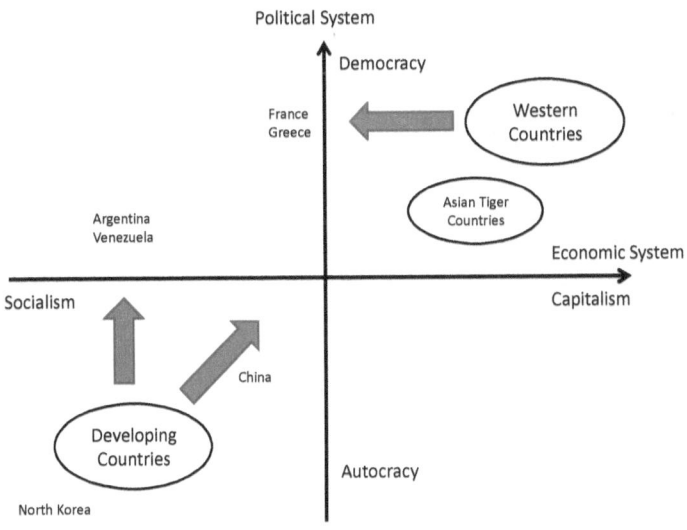

Figure 2 Economic/Political System: Geopolitical Trends

Today, European countries such as Greece and France have arguably already crossed the dividing line between capitalism and socialism while still managing to maintain democracy. On the other hand, Latin American countries such as Argentina and Venezuela reached the same socialist-democratic regime in a completely different way. They retained socialism while introducing democracy. As its private-sector economy grows more in scale and importance, China is increasingly more capitalistic and less socialistic, which in turns loosens its political system.

The Compatibility between Political and Economic Systems

Not every economic system can be compatible with every political system. Capitalism, for example, can only thrive under sufficient freedom and liberty. Indeed, modern history has provided few examples of capitalism that coexisted with autocratic political systems for an extended period of time. On the other hand, history has provided ample examples of socialism with autocracy.

Socialism coupled with democracy is a relatively new phenomenon. In Greece and other Western European countries that are rapidly evolving toward that regime, capitalism is gradually eroded as governments become increasingly intrusive in private economy in response to ever-growing populism. Latin American countries, on the other hand, reached the socialism-democracy regime by overthrowing dictators while maintaining public ownership of enterprises. One of the most important points of this book, derived from both empirical observations as well as theoretical arguments, is that democracy, when combined with socialism, is inherently dangerous and unsustainable. This explains the social and economic stress we are witnessing today in countries such as Greece, Argentina, and Venezuela. In the years and decades to come, many other countries, including America and Western European countries, will find themselves in the same dilemma as their capitalism faces further erosion and their countries become more socialistic. On the other hand, China, as its private economy continues to grow, will soon face the difficult decision of how to deal with the constraint its political system places on its vibrant private-sector economy.

2 THE SHORTCOMINGS OF DEMOCRACY

The Significance of Equal Rights

Based on the definition of democracy in chapter 1, the most important element of democracy is the equal rights all eligible citizens have, regardless of their unequal contributions to society. A person who has made great positive contributions to society has the same democratic rights as one who has made no—or even negative—contributions to society.

Political power and money can both grow in a self-reinforcing way. A person in power can often utilize his or her existing power to become even more powerful, and a person with a sufficient amount of wealth can use his or her current wealth to become even wealthier. If those positive feedback loops were allowed to grow without any constraints, then society would eventually become a politically dictatorial system and an economically monopolistic system. History shows that political dictators and economic monopolies are often very closely related. Frequently, they are actually the same entity. Their interrelationships and interdependence constitute what we call corruption.

Democracy provides a mechanism to prevent dictatorship, as the majority will always be able to vote a potential dictator out of power. Antitrust laws and progressive tax policies are designed to prevent monopolies and the excessive concentration of wealth.

Capitalism and Democracy

Because of its emphasis on rights, but not responsibilities, of each citizen, democracy by itself is not a sustainable and self-sufficient political system on which a society can be built. For a society to survive and prosper, many social functions need to be fulfilled. Goods need to be produced, and services need to be provided. Infrastructure needs to be built and maintained, rules and laws need to be created and enforced, and younger generations need to be educated. All these social functions require citizens to contribute individually and collectively, and this requirement forms the basic obligation and responsibility a citizen has to society.

A society will inevitably disintegrate if too many of its citizens fail to fulfill their basic social obligations. How do we incentivize people to fulfill their basic obligations in a democratic society? The answer is capitalism. Capitalism augments democracy by providing economic incentives for people to work. Individually, the work of each person provides a means of living, and collectively, those people contribute to the entire society.

Socialism and Democracy

While capitalism augments democracy by incentivizing people to work and makes society stronger, the combination of socialism and democracy is extremely dangerous, and over time, it will destroy society.

In a socialist society, businesses are owned by the government rather than by individuals. This public ownership makes nearly every worker a government employee. However, in a democratic society, the people also elect government officials. This circular relationship between government and people, in the sense that people elect government officials but the government also employs and pays people, creates a situation that makes it mutually beneficial for government and people to bribe each other. As a result, politicians who make the biggest promises tend to get elected and reelected, and in return, people are continually granted seemingly free benefits from the government. Such mutual bribery might face objections and resentment from the private segments of the economy in a capitalist society, but it becomes self-reinforcing in a socialist society because there are no other forces that can counter its growth. This self-reinforcing, mutually beneficial bribery process can persist for a long time without much interruption, creating illusions that such prosperity can last forever. Meanwhile, morals and productivity erode, government finances deteriorate, and debt piles up until such time that the government can no longer fund itself in the bond market.

In principle, the tendency for mutual bribery between politicians and voters has always existed in any democratic society, but several historical factors have played important roles in suppressing its emergence. This includes the historically limited influence of the government, the different philosophical views among politicians, and the attitude toward government aid among citizens. Situations today are vastly different from when America was still a relatively young country. Since the Great Depression and World War II, the US federal government has become much bigger and more influential in our private lives. The backgrounds of elected officials have also changed. While senators and representatives used to receive no pay for their public services, today we have career politicians whose livelihoods depend on whether they can be reelected. People used to be more reluctant to receive government assistance during the Great Depression. Today, most people regard government aid as their right.

What is playing out today in Europe, especially Greece, demonstrates the perils of combining democracy with socialism. By now, the pattern should be clear. It starts with politicians making too many unrealistic promises to the people in order to win votes, but because of the lack of productivity and competitiveness under the socialist system, the government usually finds itself lacking revenue to fulfill all these promises. As the economy deteriorates, the inability to lay off government workers and trim their wages and benefits makes government finances worse. More often than not, the easiest way out is resorting to debt in order to keep citizens happy. This process can last for a long time, and debt gradually piles up. Then, one day, the bond market wakes up, and investors realize it is going to be very hard for the government to meet all those debt obligations. Suddenly, the source of government funding shuts down. The government defaults on its debt, and layoffs, wage and benefit cuts, and higher taxes are then forced on people. This stirs much public resentment, and social unrest follows. This social unrest makes society even less productive and further worsens the government's finances, and eventually society disintegrates.

Political Equality and Economic Equality

People enjoy political equality within democratic societies because they have equal rights regardless of their unequal social contributions. While capitalism has created great prosperity for Western democracies, it is also responsible for creating great economic inequality between different classes of people. Progressive tax laws and antitrust regulations have ameliorated the problem of excessive concentration of wealth, but they have not totally eliminated economic inequality.

Socialism aims to achieve more economic equality by giving the means of production, and therefore the profits derived from such production, to the state. Socialist democracies have the noble goal of achieving both political and economic equality in society. The incompatibility between socialism and democracy, as has been argued in the proceeding section, shows that political equality and economic equality cannot be achieved at the same time. This observation, while disappointing, resembles the uncertainty principle in physics, which asserts that the position and velocity of a quantum particle cannot be accurately measured at the same time. We will discuss this concept more in chapter 4.

Majority Rule

Democracy means the majority rules. When a decision has to be made but different opinions emerge, the decision the majority favors prevails.

This majority rule, while fundamentally important to democracy, does not always ensure that the ultimate decisions are always right. Indeed, history is full of examples, ranging from scientific discovery, politics, and investing, that demonstrate how the majority can often be wrong. For example, when Nicolaus Copernicus first postulated that the earth was not the center of the universe and instead revolved around the sun, he was widely ridiculed. Hitler and the Nazi Party rose to power in a democratic system with the support of the majority of German people. Late-1990s investors, confident in the new-era economy and Internet wonders, drove Internet stocks to absurd levels of valuations before the bubble crashed.

There are two main reasons the majority can be wrong, and both are deeply wired into our human nature. The first comes from the fact that humans have the strong tendency to avoid short-term pains at the expense of long-term gains. We frequently take the easy path while delaying the tough decisions. Economist James Galbraith put it more bluntly: "There is no reason to believe that the democratic decision made by the living in the face of their present needs and desires will be the decision that would maximize the chance of long-term system survival. The unpleasant conclusion is that it is possible for a society to choose economic collapse."[5]

The second reason is due to herding. In general, the majority is more prone to be wrong if groupthink influences people. Rather than thinking independently and voting with the best conscience, people vote by group association, such as by race, religion, gender, unions, or political parties. When this happens, society often suffers, and the consequences can be severe or even devastating. On the other hand, when each citizen conducts decision processes independently with the best conscience, the majority is more likely to be right, and society benefits.

Freedom and Democracy

Freedom and democracy are often spoken about in the same sentences and regarded as equivalent, but they are totally different concepts. In the United States, it is the US Constitution, not the rules of democracy, that guarantees the basic freedoms, such as freedom of speech, freedom of religion, freedom of political association, and freedom of property rights. Without such constitutional protection, the rights of the minority are constantly at the mercy of the majority. The recent development in Egypt provides an example. After the Arab Spring, the Muslim Brotherhood won the democratic election and formed the government. They then followed to pass an Islamic-tilted constitution. This was against the wishes of other segments of the population with other religious beliefs.

---

[5] James K. Galbraith, *The End of Normal: The Great Crisis and the Future of Growth* (New York: Simon & Schuster, 2015), 104.

Situations like this inevitably create deep divisions among the people, and the consequent conflicts and violence further divide society. Indeed, Egyptian military had to intervene when the deep division and violence became too big of a threat to the stability of the country.

Therefore, while democracy provides a mechanism for people to rid themselves of autocratic rulers, it does not always produce a fair and free society. A democratic society without broad constitutionally guaranteed freedom is a dangerous and unstable society. Democracy simply will not work when society becomes highly polarized and the differences between factions of people become irreconcilable. When the majority imposes its will on the minority, which fundamentally violates the freedom of the minority, democracy becomes a form of tyranny of the majority. The following quote, often attributed to Thomas Jefferson but not actually verified, nevertheless presents a blunt yet accurate diagnosis of the potential perils of democracy: "A democracy is nothing more than mob rule, where 51 percent of the people may take away the rights of the other 49."[6]

The Fragile Democracy

Like a bird in an open cage that will eventually find its way out, democracy will eventually deteriorate. There are many ways such deterioration can happen.

- Democracy will erode and eventually fail when citizens collectively can no longer make wise and intelligent decisions when participating in societal governance. This might be either because of a general lack of basic education or because of widespread extreme economic hardship. As a result, citizens make poor choices about their leaders and policies. This is particularly relevant today in America as our public schools, especially those in disadvantaged neighborhoods, fail to produce qualified workforces for today's economy.

- When more than 50 percent of the voters rely in one way or another on government financial assistance, democracy enters the perilous zone of self-reinforcing feedback loops, in which the party that promises the most will always get elected, and elections degenerate into contests of who can promise the most, regardless of the feasibility of those promises. Invariably, an increasingly aggressive income and wealth transfer from the rich

---

[6] "Democracy Is Nothing More Than Mob Rule...," Monticello, n.d., http://www.monticello.org/site/jefferson/democracy-nothing-more-mob-rule.

to the poor and the able to the less able fund these promises. When that source of revenue is exhausted, the government becomes in debt. As more and more people are trapped by the lure of the seemingly free government handouts, government finances deteriorate, and debt spirals out of control.

- Democracy will fail when society chooses the path of socialism. The uncompetitive nature of such an economic system causes moral hazards among the people that will eventually force government to borrow in order to fund various social programs, putting society's future in the hands of the bond market.

- Democracy will not work without a broad-based constitution that guarantees the basic rights of the minority. This prevents the tyranny of the majority.

- Polarization is the advanced symptom that a democracy can no longer function fairly and properly. Such polarization can originate from different religious beliefs, such as in many Middle Eastern countries; traditional ethnic divides, such as in some Eastern European countries; or increasingly diverging political ideology, which is more and more prevalent in America today.

Our founders were well aware of democracy's tendency to degenerate over time and the potential threat it could pose to liberty and freedom. John Adams once wrote, "Remember, democracy never lasts long. It soon wastes, exhausts, and murders itself. There never was a democracy yet that did not commit suicide." Alexander Hamilton, commenting on liberty versus democracy, wrote, "Real liberty is never found in despotism or in the extremes of Democracy." Similarly, James Madison wrote, "democracies have ever been spectacles of turbulence and contention; have ever been found incompatible with personal security or the rights of property; and have in general been as short in their lives as they have been violent in their deaths."

3 THE CONSEQUENCES OF ASYMMETRIC RISK AND REWARD

The Concept of Asymmetric Risk and Reward

When an event's various possible outcomes bring only rewards but no losses, we say such an event has asymmetric risk and reward. Getting a free lottery ticket is an example of asymmetric risk and reward because the ticket holder can never experience any losses but faces potential gains.

When an investment has upside potential but no downside risk, investors can effectively earn risk-free returns on this investment, and parties on the opposite side of this trade are sure losers. In a freely functioning market, the price of such investment will adjust higher, and the risk and reward will quickly become more balanced.

The ability of the free market to make rapid price adjustments regarding these asymmetric risk-and-reward opportunities is crucial in maintaining long-term market stability and avoiding large-scale wealth transfer among market participants. However, such rapid adjustment is not always possible in politics and other aspects of social life. This is either because of the difficulty in recognizing these asymmetric risk-and-reward situations by the citizens or, more commonly, because of the intended and unintended consequences of government interventions and manipulations. When this happens, taxpayers are sure losers, and the huge price tag a society faces will eventually destabilize its foundation.

Asymmetric Risk and Reward for Wall Street Bankers

The reckless behavior of Wall Street banks leading up to the 2007–2008 financial crisis provides the most recent example of asymmetric risk and reward. This behavior enriched Wall Street bankers at the expense of bank shareholders and, ultimately, American taxpayers. When a banker undertakes a position either in the form of a loan or a complex derivative trade, the banker is usually rewarded handsomely (in the form of annual bonuses) from the income streams derived from such a position. However, when these positions blow up many years down the road, the worst that can happen to the banker is he or she gets fired (if the banker is still around). It is extremely rare to see any recall of past bonuses. Such asymmetric risk and reward is inherent in the eat-what-you-kill culture of Wall Street, but the situation has worsened since the 1980s and 1990s. That was when Wall Street firms transformed themselves from private partnerships to publically traded companies. As private partnerships, because their own capital was at risk, senior partners presumably were more prudent in their dealings and more attentive to their risks. As publically traded firms, however, winnings were shared with the bankers, while losses completely went to shareholders and even taxpayers. It was only a matter of time before disaster occurred.

The victims of this asymmetric risk and reward range from bank shareholders to Main Street citizens. Following the financial crisis of 2008, many workers' jobs were eliminated. Homeowners nationwide experienced large drops in their home values, and many even lost their homes to foreclosures. Ordinary investors saw their lifetime savings quickly evaporate. In response, corporations adopted near-panic cost-cutting measures. In its 2009 fiscal second-quarter earnings release, for example, FedEx announced a pay cut of 20 percent for CEO Fred Smith, 7.5 percent to 10 percent for senior executives, and 5 percent for other US-based salaried exempt personnel. In addition, 2009 merit-based salary increases for US salaried exempt personnel were eliminated, and 2009 401(k) company-matching contributions were suspended. At the same time, Merrill Lynch bankers, after losing $27 billion in 2008, carved out $3.6 billion in year-end bonuses for themselves right before the firm was sold to Bank of America.[7] One cannot find more contrast between Main Street and Wall Street.

Asymmetric Risk and Reward for Investors
Throughout the decade leading up to the financial crisis of 2007–2008, banks, in their quest for more profits, became more levered in their balance sheets and aggressive with their many "innovations" of exotic instruments. There was a growing unspoken confidence among Wall Street players that if things went wrong, then the Fed would come in and bail them out. Indeed, the Fed had never let Wall Street down. After the stock market crash of October 1987, Fed Chairman Alan Greenspan came to the rescue by injecting massive amounts of liquidity into the market, and the market quickly recovered. The collapse of Long-Term Capital Management caused another Fed-engineered rescue, which pushed the market higher. This helped it finish its final leg of the bull market during the Internet bubble. After the burst of the Internet bubble and the 9/11 terrorist attacks, the Fed did its magic once again. This time, it lowered interest rates to nearly zero and kept them there for an

---

[7] "Big Bonuses for Many at Merrill, Cuomo Says," DealBook, *New York Times*, February 11, 2009, http://dealbook.nytimes.com/2009/02/11/big-bonuses-for-many-at-merrill-cuomo-says/comment-page-4/.

extended period of time, thus sowing the seed for the ultimate bubble in the housing market.

This asymmetric risk and reward, in the sense that banks and investors profited when things went well but the Fed came to the rescue when things went wrong, took a long time to develop and firmly imprint in the minds of investors. It first took form when famed investor Martin Zweig coined the phrase "don't fight the Fed" in the 1980s. Because economic cycles usually take years to play out, economic panics don't come that often, and the Fed used to work secretively, so investors' reliance on the Fed wasn't always as high as today. However, the Fed has become more predictable since the early 1990s. That was when Greenspan made the Fed more transparent, and after repeated "successful" Fed rescues, investors' confidence in the Fed grew as time went on. Their behavior then became more aggressive and reckless, which eventually led to the near-collapse of the entire financial system in the fall of 2008.

Today, after being bailed out by the Fed one more time through a combination of zero interest rates and multiple rounds of asset purchases, investors' reliance on and confidence in the Fed has reached unprecedented heights. Apparently, the best lesson investors learned from the 2008 financial crisis can be paraphrased as the following: if an event, when it happens, would have such devastating consequences that it would bring down the entire system, then such an event won't happen. Indeed, the Fed would never allow it to take place.

In this game of Fed-engineered asymmetric risk and reward, conservative savers have been the losers. Near-zero interest rates on fixed income instruments made it extremely difficult for savers to earn a reasonable return, and senior citizens found it impossible to live off interest income from their lifetime savings. Some had to eat into their principals, while others were forced to seek riskier investments. History has yet to tell how this will ultimately unfold.

Asymmetric Risk and Reward for Real Estate Owners

Residential real estate in the United States is another example of asymmetric risk and reward derived from government distortions. To demonstrate this, let us look at the following comparison between residential real estate and stocks.

- Mortgage interest on residential real estate is tax deductible, while margin cost on stocks is subject to the 2 percent limitation rule for most investors.
- Mortgage interest rates are usually much lower than broker margin rates thanks to government-sponsored entities, such as

Fannie Mae and Freddie Mac, which had to be rescued by taxpayers in 2008.

- Capital gains on owner-occupied residential real estate are tax exempt up to $500,000 for couples, while capital gains on stocks are always taxable.
- Residential real estate can be bought with a very low down payment, but stock margins are typically capped at 50 percent for most investors.
- Homeowners who are behind on their mortgage interest payments cannot be easily evicted, while stock investors who fail to meet margin calls will see their stocks immediately liquidated.
- Homeowners with negative equity values can legally walk away, and lenders take the loss. Brokers can go after stock investors with negative account values.

With so many advantages, housing became a hot speculative vehicle in the decade leading up to the 2007–2008 financial crisis. After the crisis, with government intervention, many delinquent homeowners were able to reduce their mortgage principals and lower their interest payments, turning mortgage bond investors and taxpayers into losers.

Asymmetric Risk and Reward for Politicians

Politicians and elected officials represent another example of asymmetric risk and reward. This stems from the fact that policy effects (either good or bad) usually take a long time to be realized. Most likely this is long after the elected officials leave office. In contrast, the need to get more votes and win reelection is urgent and immediate. Therefore, there is little incentive to implement policies that are beneficial long term to society but unhelpful to reelections, while there are all the incentives to adopt policies that might gain them more votes and win them reelection—regardless of their long-term effect on the community or society. Such asymmetry is the major reason why governments at all levels today, from federal to state to local, not to mention those in troubled European countries, are facing severe financial crises that threaten to destroy the fundamental fabric of Western nations.

When elected officials hand out impractical promises to voters and yield to the demand of special interest groups, such as public-sector unions, in order to win votes, eventually such practices will provide disincentives to work and cripple the financial health of the government. These elected officials, along with the special interest groups, are the winners, but taxpayers are the losers. After retirement, the nice packages of pensions and benefits they receive are independent of their contributions, whether positive or negative, to the community or society. The relationships they build while in office make them valuable candidates on corporate boards or as hotly sought-after lobbyists, while their ill-conceived decisions become burdens to their successors and taxpayers.

Asymmetric Risk and Reward in Democracy

Democracy, because of its guarantee of equal rights without any requirements or responsibilities of the citizens, is inherently a fragile system due to this asymmetry between rights and responsibilities. As more and more people take advantage of their guaranteed rights without contributing to society, society cannot sustain itself, and it deteriorates gradually. Ultimately, this leads to social chaos and disintegration.

Capitalism, as argued in chapter 2, can save democracy by providing incentives for people to work. Socialism, on the other hand, is extremely dangerous when combined with democracy.

> A democracy cannot exist as a permanent form of government. It can only exist until voters discover that they can vote themselves largesse from the Public Treasury. From that moment on, the majority always votes for the candidates promising the most benefits from the Public Treasury, with the result that a democracy always collapses over loose fiscal policy, always followed by dictatorship.

It is still much debated whether the preceding quotation on democracy is truly attributable to Fraser Tytler (1747–1813). Regardless of who actually said this, it accurately reflects one of the fundamental flaws of democracy. Indeed, the recent European debt crisis is a perfect manifestation. Organized in the form of powerful unions, in both the public sector and the private sector, European workers have routinely favored socialist candidates who promised them largess funded not by real economic growth but government debt. The fact that such debt-financed prosperity can keep going for years and even decades creates the illusion that such prosperity is real and sustainable, but eventually, the bond market panics after investors realize the levels of government debt are unsustainable. This happened in countries such as Greece, Portugal, Italy, and Spain. In those instances, the source of government funding suddenly evaporated, and these countries had to be bailed out. It was only after Mario Draghi, the European Central Bank president, promised to do "whatever it takes" that the bond market began to temporarily settle down. However, with mere monetary trickeries, such as quantitative easing and negative interest rates without real political reforms, the final verdict for those socialist democracies is yet to come.

Conclusion

When bad decisions and irresponsible behavior bear no or insufficient consequences to those who engage in such decisions and behavior, it is certain that such bad decisions and behavior will recur—most likely with increasing scale and frequency. This will happen until the people making the bad decisions have incurred so much social damage that people finally wake up and revolt.

4 SHORT-TERM ORDER VERSUS LONG-TERM FRAGILITY

Heisenberg's Uncertainty Principle

Heisenberg's uncertainty principle states that the position and velocity of a quantum particle cannot be known with infinite accuracy at the same time. A precise knowledge of its position comes at the expense of the knowledge of its velocity—and vice versa.

Both nature and human society exhibit a similar property in the sense that short-term order and long-term stability cannot be achieved at the same time. Excessively maintaining strict short-term order leads to nearly certain long-term failures.[8] The following examples will demonstrate this principle.

The Story of Yu the Great

In ancient China, the heartland was frequently plagued with floods, which hampered economic growth and threatened lives. Yu's father, Gun, was tasked with controlling the flood. Gun's method for flood control was simple and intuitive: he tried to block the water from overflowing by building many dikes along the rivers. This method, while successful in preventing many small floods, eventually failed when there was too much water for the dikes to hold. What was worse, the extra amount of water accumulated by the dikes made the flood even more powerful and devastating.

When Yu took over the task of fighting the flood from his father, he decided to adopt a different approach. Instead of building dikes to block the water, he dug many irrigation canals to channel the water into fields. This relieved the water pressure and turned out to be a great success. Although small-scale floods would occasionally take place from those numerous canals, they were never so powerful to cause a lot of damage. The devastating big floods were avoided. As a result of Yu's effort, ancient Chinese civilization was able to flourish along those major rivers.

The story of Yu the Great is instructive. In the battle against floods, one cannot eliminate both small floods and big floods at the same time. Yu's father tried to block the water from overflowing. While he was able to contain many small floods, he failed with the big floods. Yu, by allowing small floods to take place, was able to avoid the devastating big floods.

---

[8] Nassim Taleb discusses this concept more in his book *Antifragile: Things That Gain from Disorder* (New York: Random House, 2014).

The Role of Prescribed Fire in Forest Protection[9]

One of the best ways to protect forests from devastating fire and disease is, ironically, prescribed burning. Prescribed fire benefits the forest in many ways. It removes fuel loads, such as dead wood, dry leaves, and pine needles accumulated over a long period of time, thus reducing the intensity of fire that can destroy the entire forest. It also maintains the balance and diversity of plant populations in the forest. After prescribed burning, food for wildlife increases, and there is more growth of flowers, seeds, and fruits.

The benefits of controlled burning have not always been widely recognized and accepted. Indeed, in the beginning of the twentieth century, the US Forest Service maintained a firm policy against burning. State forestry agencies that allowed controlled burning saw their federal funding withheld. The Smokey Bear program, a campaign against fire, became extremely effective. Created by the National Advertising Council, the US Forest Service, and state forestry agencies, it featured Smokey Bear urging people to be careful with fire.

Mostly due to those fire suppression and prevention campaigns and activities, there was a decrease in frequency and acreage of fires throughout much of the twentieth century. This resulted in changes in forest ecosystems, including denser underbrush, accumulation of live and dead vegetation, and more invasive plants. Most ironically, while the frequency of fires was reduced, wildfires actually became more damaging due to the abundance of accumulated fuel.

The lesson we can draw from prescribed fire is again very instructive. Controlled burning removes fuel and makes forests safer and healthier over the long term, while strictly disallowing any fire increases the risk of big fires that might destroy the forest and actually has negative effects on the forest ecosystem.

Open, Free Society versus Closed, Autocratic Society

An open and free society can often seem chaotic. Diversity of opinions means endless dialogue and debate. Citizens who disagree with certain aspects of government policies might organize themselves and demonstrate on the street. Government rules and regulations often have to go through lengthy periods of discussion before they can go into effect. Legislative processes are usually long and tedious. Government administrations at different levels change regularly as officials are elected into and out of office. Despite these changes, one thing remains

---

[9] Nassim Taleb discusses this topic extensively in his various articles and speeches.

constant—the US Constitution. The US Constitution provides a mechanism for people to change the government they dislike and choose the government they like, thus making violent revolutions unnecessary. Such political systems are self-sustainable and have lasting longevity.

A closed and autocratic society can seem very orderly. Public opinions are usually very uniform and dominated by government doctrines, which leaves little room for dialogue and debate. Dissent against government is suppressed, and political associations and demonstrations are strictly disallowed. Government actions are always speedy and have little opportunity for discussions, and the head of the government usually stays in power until his or her death. The lack of mechanisms for people to peacefully choose their own government means that the only way to change is through violent revolution. Such political systems are fragile and will eventually fail.

A closed autocratic society, by keeping strict social order to maintain its rule, is doomed to fail in the long run because violent revolution is the only way for people to change the government. On the other hand, an open and free society has longevity because it empowers people to choose their own government within the framework of the Constitution. This makes violent revolution unnecessary.

The Perils of Central Banks

The US Congress created the Federal Reserve System after the enactment of the Federal Reserve Act of 1913. Its original purpose was to create a federal currency to avoid the repeated financial panics caused by bank runs between 1873 and 1907. However, the Humphrey-Hawkins Full Employment Act of 1978 significantly changed the Fed's mandate. Instead of preventing financial panics and bank runs, the Fed was also tasked with promoting the dual goal of maximum employment and price stability.

Since 1978, the Federal Reserve's track record in achieving this dual mandate has been mixed at best. A more complete review of the Fed's recent history has demonstrated that now that we have had more time to examine the long-term effect of these policy decisions, the perceived harms or benefits of the Fed's actions have changed. For example, Paul Volcker's Fed was extremely controversial when it raised the federal funds rate to a peak of 20 percent in June 1981, causing unemployment rates to top 10 percent and a deep recession to commence. In protest, farmers drove their tractors into Washington, DC, and blockaded the Marriner S. Eccles Building, which housed the Federal Reserve Board. Today, after more than thirty years, the merits of Volcker's preemptive interest rate policy are better understood and appreciated. Paul Volcker is now widely recognized as one of the best Federal Reserve chairmen and is credited with ending the decade-long stagflation. In contrast, Alan Greenspan, who succeeded Paul Volcker as Fed chairman in 1987, enjoyed great popularity throughout his tenure. His decisions to cut the federal funds rate after the market crash in 1987, the collapse of Long-Term Capital Management in 1998, and the 9/11 terrorist attacks in 2001 stabilized the market in each case. He was so popular that he received wide praise from both sides of the aisle in his last testimony to Congress, and some senators went so far as to say that when he left, we needed to erect his statue just to scare off inflation. Today, however, after enduring the greatest financial crisis since the Great Depression, what was once unquestionable is now worth pondering. Were the seeds of the crisis not sowed during those booming years of the Greenspan era? Did each of the market rescues not only waste opportunities to cleanse the market excesses but also embolden investors to take greater risks, which resulted in even bigger bubbles? Did the effort to smooth out short-term fluctuations in the economy, via the manipulations of interest rates and the markets, not jeopardize the long-term economic stability of this nation?

What has the Fed really achieved by raising interest rates when the economy is perceived to be too strong and cutting interest rates when the economy shows signs of softening? Has it made the economic growth steadier and smoother? The answer might have been yes in 1995, after the Fed had engineered a slowdown of the economy in 1994 by raising rates aggressively and avoided a recession in 1995 by reversing some of its previous actions. However, in view of the two greatest bubbles in the short span of a decade and the most severe financial crisis since the Great Depression, the answer seems to be a resounding no. By manipulating interest rates and the markets, the Fed was able to temporarily smooth out some short-term fluctuations at the expense of creating even more devastating bubbles later. The Fed might have won a series of small battles, but it lost the big war by not being able to recognize and prevent the financial crisis whose seeds it had sown in the first place.

The final fate of the Fed's policy is now in the hands of Chairwoman Yellen and her future successors. After multiple rounds of quantitative easing, stock prices have reached an all-time high, and the housing market has finally shown clear signs of recovery. Investors, however, are at risk of the ultimate bubble—their seemingly infinite faith in (and reliance on) the Federal Reserve. Very few people seem to be bothered by the thought that the future of our democracy now rests on the outcome of an unproven and risky monetary experiment, and the people who are in charge of such policy today are unelected officials who, with their collective wisdom, did not see this financial crisis coming in the first place.

Conclusion

Historical evidence has demonstrated that excessively suppressing short-term fluctuations can cause nearly certain long-term systemic failures. Small-scale volatility is beneficial because it constantly reminds participants of prudence and caution, forcing adjustments that might be unpleasant in the short term but that are beneficial in the long run. Without such frequent but modest adjustments, excesses and inefficiencies are not cleansed, cautions are thrown out, and moral hazards grow. Questionable projects are funded and undertaken, and leverage increases as participants become overly complacent and even reckless. The subsequent shocks and adjustments become particularly painful and even devastating, as we witnessed during and after the financial crisis of 2008.

Viewed in this regard, the current goals of central banks are futile, and their activities actually pose great threat to the long-term financial and political stability of our society.

5 THE DANGER OF POLARIZATION

The Changing American Society

Over the last two hundred years, American society has greatly changed both socially and politically. This happened as people's views and moral standards evolved over time. Children used to spend entire Sundays in church schools. Today, they mostly use Sundays to catch up on homework or sleep, play their favorite sports or video games, and maybe make a brief visit to the church. Same-sex marriage, once a social taboo, is now socially acceptable and has become legal with the most recent Supreme Court ruling. Eugene Victor Debs ran unsuccessfully for president as a Socialist Party candidate no less than five times and was considered radical in his day. Among his many ideas were abolishment of child labor, women's right to vote, and a more equitable tax system. Today, these are such basic elements of our society that we take them for granted.

Social changes are gradual, and they are irresistible and irreversible because they represent the will of the people. Although the shifts of views can be tremendous, they do not cause disruption or instability to society. Their long-term influence on society, however, is still largely unclear. Some, such as William Ophuls,[10] labeled those social changes as part of society's moral decay, which eventually would lead to the failure of our civilization. Others herald them as the sign of progress of our time. Either way, when the majority of the people change their attitudes, society moves forward peacefully. However, when a society is deeply divided and split over an important issue, the resulting polarization can be very destabilizing, and the end result can be unpredictable.

Therefore, our political leaders would be wise to take the temperature of society when they push for social changes based on their own political ideologies. Pushing for social changes when society is not ready and citizens are still deeply divided runs the risk of splitting and destabilizing the nation, while pushing for social changes in a way that allows ample time for rigorous and honest debate ultimately maintains unity and preserves our democracy.

Phase Transition

In physics, a phase transition is matter's change of state in response to changes in external conditions. For example, ice changes into water as

---

[10] William Ophuls, *Immoderate Greatness: Why Civilizations Fail* (North Charleston, SC: CreateSpace, 2012).

temperatures rise above the freezing point, and as temperatures continue to rise, water further changes into vapor.

One of the most-studied phase transitions in physics involves ferromagnetism, where ferromagnetic materials become magnetized as temperatures drop below a certain critical point. With the aid of the Ising model, first studied by German physicist Ernst Ising in the 1920s, we have gained much insight into such physical phenomena. Magnetism is formed when molecular magnetic spins align themselves in the same direction, and the ability for such alignment not only depends on the strength of interactions between molecular magnetic spins but also on the extent of connectedness among themselves. For example, in the one-dimensional Ising model with finite-range interactions, where magnetic spins form a one-dimensional chain and each only interacts with a finite number of other magnetic spins, magnetism is not possible, and phase transition will never occur at finite temperatures. By putting these magnetic spins on a simple two-dimensional square lattice and allowing them only to interact with their nearest neighbors, we find that magnetism becomes possible, and phase transition occurs at a certain nonzero temperature.

The fact that a one-dimensional Ising chain with long but finite range interactions cannot produce magnetism via phase transitions but a two-dimensional Ising lattice with only nearest-neighbor interactions is able to produce magnetism via phase transitions indicates that the extent of connectedness among the molecular spins plays a crucial role in enabling phase transitions. This important insight gained from the Ising model has significant implications for understanding a vast array of social phenomena. Investment bubbles, for example, arise because of the herding behaviors among investors. This is where investors strongly influence one another, resulting in consensus on the merits of an investment regardless of the high price.

The Role of Social Media

Insights gained from the study of the Ising model on phase transitions can help us better understand the role of social media in our society today. Social media greatly increases the connectedness among the people. As a result, it is much easier for people to get organized. The importance of the ability to organize became very clear during the Arab Spring, as nearly spontaneous rebellions in Tunisia, Libya, and Egypt were able to change governments in those countries relatively quickly. Social media tilts the power away from the government and large corporations in favor of the people, and it greatly quickens the pace of social changes. As a result, society becomes more volatile and more susceptible to large-scale changes and even revolution.

The Vulnerability of Traditional Institutions

The ability for people to organize, facilitated by social media and mobile technology, has created a new business model of shared economy. This is poised to disrupt the traditional business model of corporations. In the travel and lodging industry, we have seen the rise of Uber and Airbnb, and in the consumer lending business, there are now peer-to-peer lending platforms. Perhaps no industry has witnessed more disruptions than traditional media, where numerous online news and entertainment websites and countless YouTube channels compete with traditional newspapers and televisions daily. Today's consumers, especially millennials, are no longer hostage to traditional newspapers and television news programs, and political biases embedded in these newspapers and television programs can no longer influence people as easily as they used to. Never before in history have people been more connected and empowered and corporations and institutions more vulnerable.

Correlation and Polarization

The study of the Ising model reveals that as the temperature approaches the critical transition point, magnetic spins become more and more correlated. They form larger and larger clusters inside which magnetic spins are aligned in the same direction. The size of these clusters, which physicists call correlation length, becomes infinite as the temperature reaches the critical transition point.

Similarly, as a society gets closer to the boiling point of a social conflict, it becomes increasingly polarized as citizens form large political blocs based on their ideologies. There are fewer and fewer politically independent citizens who, under more normal and less polarizing circumstances, would be able to guide society along the middle path. As a result, democracy can no longer function well, and society becomes particularly vulnerable and unstable. The country might split peacefully, or democracy could become a form of tyranny of the majority.

Political Polarization in America Today

During good economic times, when the rising tide lifts all boats, people at different levels of economic stratification usually understand that cooperation is mutually beneficial. However, during tougher times, the economy becomes more of a zero-sum game, where the gains for capital frequently have to come at the expense of labor—and vice versa. It therefore becomes more difficult for labor and capital to cooperate, and social stress and political polarization become more prominent.

There are many signs that American society has become more politically polarized in recent decades, and such polarization has seemingly become particularly acute since the financial crisis of 2008. That was where a soaring stock market, due largely to the zero interest rate policy by the Fed, and the sluggish labor market and stagnant wages, due largely to global trade and international competitions, worsened the income and wealth inequality. As more and more households experience financial difficulties and national debt reaches worrisome levels, Americans have become more divided on major issues, such as tax fairness, fiscal responsibility, education, and health-care inequality.

Recent studies have largely confirmed this trend. Moreover, they reveal that such divisiveness has become deeply entrenched in our political processes. A recent Pew Research Center report[11] indicated that an increasing percentage of the population now holds strong ideological views. This appeared on both sides of the political spectrum. Furthermore, these people tend to be more actively engaged in the political process. As a result, Americans are electing more partisan senators and representatives to the US Congress, which in turn has become increasingly more divided and less productive. The 2016 election, in which voters provided surprisingly strong support for Donald Trump and Bernie Sanders, is further evidence of this phenomenon.

A separate study by Clio Andris and others provides further quantitative evidence of such partisan polarization in the House of Representatives.[12] By examining the empirical roll call records of all the members of the House of Representatives from 1949 to 2012, the authors presented convincing quantitative evidence of increasing partisanship in recent years. From the late 1970s and throughout much of the 1980s, the study found that House representatives routinely crossed party lines and voted for legislation the other party sponsored. This bipartisan cooperation has eroded since the 1990s. Overall cross-party disagreements in roll call votes has accelerated since the financial crisis

---

[11] "Political Polarization in the American Public," Pew Research Center, June 12, 2014, http://www.people-press.org/2014/06/12/political-polarization-in-the-american-public/.

[12] Andris, Clio, David Lee, Marcus J. Hamilton, Mauro Martino, Christian E. Gunning, and John Armistead Selden, "The Rise of Partisanship and Super-Cooperators in the US House of Representatives," *PLoS One* 10, no. 4 (2015), http://journals.plos.org/plosone/article?id=10.1371/journal.pone.0123507.

in 2008, as witnessed by a series of controversies surrounding the Affordable Care Act, the debt-ceiling and budget debate, and the government shutdown. The number of representatives involved in bipartisan cooperation remained steady prior to 2000, but it experienced a sharp drop since 2000, a year that, in many respects, marked the recent peak of economic prosperity in this country.

The Threat to Our Democracy

Based on the study by Clio Andris and others, the trend of partisanship developed throughout the period of the study (1949–2012) has greatly accelerated since 2000—and particularly since the financial crisis of 2008. In many respects, the US economic prosperity peaked around the year 2000, and I postulate that the acceleration of partisanship since 2000 is largely the result of the burst of the Internet bubble in 2000 and the burst of the housing bubble in 2008. It is understandable that the hardships many American families have experienced following the bursts of the twin bubbles have elevated partisanship. Furthermore, the rapid advances of the Internet and various social media platforms since 2000 have increased the connectedness among American people, further facilitating the polarization in our society today.

Democracy works best if citizens are objective and mutually independent when participating in the governing of society. When the population distribution resembles a bell-shaped curve dominated by the middle, societies are harmonious and stable. However, when citizens form partisan blocs with strong ideological views, the population distribution resembles a bimodal distribution with little middle ground. Such societies are polarized and highly volatile, and democracy eventually fails.

The transition from a bell-shaped population distribution to a bimodal distribution resembles phase transitions in physics in that citizens within each political bloc become highly correlated with a uniform political ideology. Instead of benefiting from a diversity of views when the middle majority dominates society, we have a confrontation of just two opposing ideologies. Such transitions might take a long time (decades) to materialize, but they can be greatly accelerated due to economic stress and increasing connectedness via social media. The exponential increase in partisanship in recent years revealed in the study by Clio Andris and others indicates that American society today is at the advanced stage of such a transition. (See figure 3.) This is the most direct threat to our democracy today.

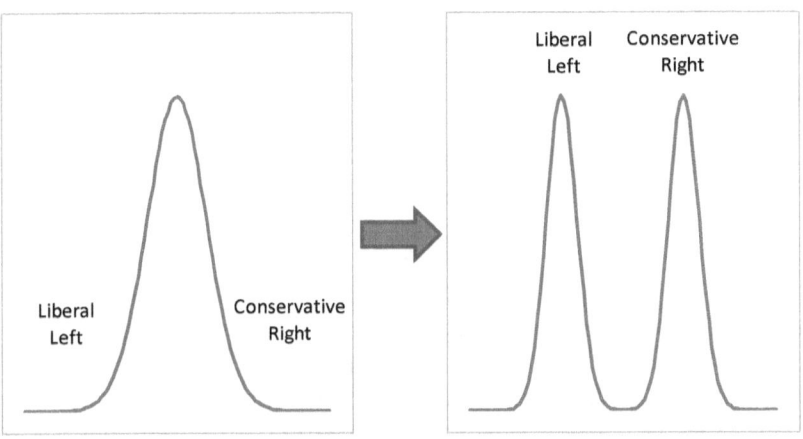

Figure 3 The Diagram of Polarization

6 THE THREAT OF PUBLIC-SECTOR EMPLOYEE UNIONS

Private-Sector Unions

Private-sector unions, despite their tumultuous history, have played a constructive role in ensuring safer work rules and fairer distribution of profits. On the other hand, corporate management, people who are paid to look after shareholders' interests and who are often significant part owners of corporations themselves, have historically done a good job of protecting the shareholders' capital and maximizing shareholders' profits. Moreover, both labor and management understand that they need each other. Labor needs capital for employment, while capital needs labor to produce goods and services for profits. Such mutual reliance provides a subtle balance between the two parties. As a result, in cases of dispute, more often than not, we can trust that a sensible compromise can be reached, and mutual self-destruction will be avoided. In the rare cases where a compromise cannot be reached, such as in the case of the bankruptcy of General Motors Company, investors were mostly wiped out, but labor also suffered devastating financial losses.

Today, memberships in private-sector unions have declined significantly from their heyday, a fact largely reflective of the decline of manufacturing in the United States and the difficulty of organizing unions among service-sector workers because of more frequent turnover.

Public-Sector Unions

In contrast to private-sector unions, public-sector unions have grown in recent decades both in their membership and in their political influence. This reflects the ever-growing government at all levels of our society today. If the justification of private-sector unions is the pursuit of safer work rules and fairer distribution of profits, then such justification does not apply to public-sector unions. First, public-sector workers, except for perhaps police officers and firefighters, mostly work in nonhazardous environments, and second, governments are not profit oriented; no government will ever subject workers to hazardous conditions in pursuit of profit. In fact, governments collectively operate at a loss today.

While corporate management has historically done a good job for shareholders and provided a counterbalance to private-sector unions, our elected officials have proven that, collectively, they have been poor stewards of taxpayers' interests. Such an outcome, however, is inherently built into the democratic process. Being one of the most vocal and best-organized political organizations, public-sector unions' support is highly sought after by politicians, and their votes often determine the outcomes in local political elections. In return for their votes, politicians make generous promises and concessions at the expense of taxpayers' long-term interests.

As a result of this corrupted conflict of interest, public-sector unions have been able to grow relatively unchecked in recent decades. There have been neither market forces nor political wills strong enough to counterbalance public-sector unions. As this goes on, governments' financial conditions deteriorate at local, state, and federal levels, and their obligations to public-sector employees' pensions grow out of control. In states and municipalities heavily dominated by public-sector unions, trying to fix this pension liability issue is often instant political suicide, and the lack of political will and incentives to fix these problems means the ultimate resolution will be in the form of a financial crisis—when bond investors are no longer willing to finance government profligacy. With the recent bankruptcy of Detroit, this process might well have begun.

Symbols of Socialism

Although it is commonly accepted that private-sector unions provide a necessary counterbalance to capital on behalf of labor, one wonders what roles the public-sector unions play. How can the public-sector unions, which represent only a small segment of the people, hijack the government, which is of the people, by the people, for the people?

The increasingly powerful public-sector unions represent the trend of our society today. We are moving away from capitalism, which has been responsible for the greatness of this nation, toward socialism, which, when combined with democracy, will eventually ruin our society. The size of public-sector unions is nothing but a measurement of the degree of socialism of our society. As our society becomes more socialistic, the size of our government increases, and so do the size and influence of public-sector unions.

Teachers' Unions

While the corruptive conflict of interest between public-sector unions and elected officials has damaged public finances, the teachers' unions are particularly harmful because they are partially responsible for the current poor status of public education. The rigid employment and compensation rules make it very hard to fire unqualified teachers and attract talented young graduates from top universities. After all, why would bright young graduates from Harvard or Stanford choose to be public school teachers when union rules dictate that their starting salary will be low and that they will be the first to be laid off because of their low union seniority? Consequently, as decades go by, the overall quality of teachers is bound to deteriorate.

The failure of our public education system today is a cancer in our society that will destabilize and eventually destroy our democracy. Students who fail in their kindergarten through twelfth-grade education are much more likely to become financial burdens to society in their later years. As our schools produce more and more unqualified workers, society will find it increasingly difficult to take care of these unemployed or unemployable citizens, and the financial burdens on society will eventually become unmanageable. Meanwhile, those unemployed or unemployable citizens will become more resentful of society, their ability to participate in the democratic governing processes becomes questionable, democracy deteriorates, and society eventually becomes politically unstable.

The Story of New York's "Success Academy Charter Schools"

Public education in America is extremely uneven. In communities that can provide adequate tax revenue to support their school districts, one often finds that the majority of teachers are qualified and dedicated. In those school districts, the outcome of education is largely dependent on student motivation and parental involvement. In economically disadvantaged school districts, where the qualifications and dedication of teachers are less uniform, learning becomes particularly challenging for students. As the public school system has deteriorated over the years, America has become a society that provides unequal opportunities to different segments of students.

Although this inequality has been widely recognized and discussed, government has proven unable to tackle this problem. Despite trillions of dollars of resources being utilized in the last several decades in the government's war on poverty, public education in economically disadvantaged areas has not shown any signs of improvement. In good times, it is easy for politicians to throw money at schools without actually making sure reforms are carried out. When lots of cities find themselves financially constrained, however, fixing their poorly run school districts becomes extremely challenging. In order to actually reform failing schools, it requires hard work by dedicated and passionate leaders who are unafraid of constant battles with teachers' unions, which are influential factors in most local political campaigns, and politicians whose political elections teachers' unions help to finance. The story of Success Academy Charter Schools in New York City provides an example of what it takes to fundamentally reform our failing school system.

From a single charter school named Harlem Success Academy in 2006, Success Academy Charter Schools has grown into an operator of more than thirty public charter schools in New York City. By all academic standards, it is a great success story. In the 2014 state exam, among all 3,560 New York State schools, schools in the Success Academy network as a whole ranked in the top 1 percent in math and the top 3 percent in English. To ensure equality of opportunity and to avoid student admission bias, Success Academy adopts a lottery system, which accepts students on a purely random basis.

With all these successes, the charter school network and its leader, Eva Moskowitz, have still faced many obstacles from different directions,[13] ranging from teachers' unions and their supporters to the newly elected mayor of New York City. Indeed, even when Eva Moskowitz was still serving as chair of New York City Council's education committee, the United Federation of Teachers regarded her as a great threat to their interests, and its members were urged to vote against her. More recently, the newly elected mayor of New York City threatened to revoke the free space to three Success Academy schools while continuing to grant free space to all other public charter schools. It was only after the intervention of New York State Governor Cuomo that the three Success Academy schools were able to continue to operate. Meanwhile, the effort to slow the growth of charter schools battles on. Charter schools in New York, for example, are only allowed to start at a very small scale, adding only one grade as each year progresses. Otherwise, teachers will have to be unionized—a regulation undoubtedly meant to protect the teachers' unions. The plan to further grow the Success Academy network faces fierce opposition from the new mayor's administration, and teachers' unions even organized and paid for demonstrations to target and intimidate financial donors to the charter school.

A Tale of Two Mayors

New York City's previous mayor, Mike Bloomberg, a man with great business successes and vast financial resources, is a living example of a leader whose financial independence allowed him to do what was right for the students rather than the special interest groups, such as teachers'

---

[13] "The Battle for New York Schools: Eva Moskowitz vs. Mayor Bill de Blasio," Daniel Bergner, *The New York Times*, September 3, 2014, http://www.nytimes.com/2014/09/07/magazine/the-battle-for-new-york-schools-eva-moskowitz-vs-mayor-bill-de-blasio.html?_r=0.

unions. Throughout his tenure as mayor, he fought many battles with the teachers' unions, and he implemented policies aimed to increase the accountability for teachers. He once famously likened an endorsement from New York City teachers' unions to a "kiss of death." His successor has a different approach. Backed by the teachers' unions, the new mayor unwound many of Mayor Bloomberg's policies. In 2014, the city granted a generous contract to the teachers' union. That was less than a month after a $350,000 donation from the American Federation of Teachers to a nonprofit run by the new mayor's advisers.

Conclusion

When an object or organization can grow without any impediment, it will keep growing until it becomes so large in scale and influence that it begins to destabilize the entire system. Public-sector employee unions, especially teachers' unions, are such organizations. Aided often by politicians they help to elect, public-sector employee unions and the entitlements and financial obligations owed to them by the federal, state, and local governments have reached such critical levels that they have begun to have a destabilizing effect on society. In the coming decade, America will have to face reality and find a fair and long-term solution for this problem. Failure to do so will seriously damage the social fabric of our society and eventually destroy our democracy.

7 THE THREAT OF DEBT

The Culture of Debt

When future historians look back at our current era, they will undoubtedly characterize the great scale of debt, both domestically and internationally. Today, our society and economy are permeated with excessive debt and liability. However, our attitude toward debt has also grown more casual over the years. Consumers regard the ability to borrow as their privilege, and politicians naturally oblige and facilitate it. Students routinely take out loans to fund their college education, but this is regardless of their ability to generate sufficient future income with their chosen careers. During the housing bubble, homeowners aggressively took out mortgages to finance the purchases of homes with the belief that house prices could only go up. Governments rely on debt to finance their projects and fill their pension gaps, but their financial projections invariably turn out too optimistic.

When the government bailed out delinquent homeowners after the housing crisis, it created moral hazards. Such moral hazards encourage further irresponsible borrowing by consumers and governments, with the help of eager lenders and investors faced with low to even negative interest rates due to central banks' monetary policies around the world. Today, the belief is growing that student debt will eventually be restructured or forgiven. Instead of facing up to the budgetary reality, governments choose to delay the day of reckoning by continuing to borrow from the bond market, thus making the problem worse and much harder to tackle in the future.

The Historical Evolution of Federal Debt

Over the last one hundred years, the amount of federal debt, both in absolute terms as well as in relative terms when compared with the GDP, has undergone great change.[14] By 2015, the US federal government had accumulated nearly $19 trillion of debt in the form of treasury bills, notes, and bonds. In addition, the federal government also faced many more obligations in the form of pensions, social security, and health-care costs. Finally, the United States also has off-balance sheet liabilities in terms of its military commitment to NATO and treaty countries, such as

---

[14] "National Debt by Year Compared to GDP and Major Events," Kimberly Amadeo, TheBalance.com, November 9, 2016, https://www.thebalance.com/national-debt-by-year-compared-to-gdp-and-major-events-3306287.

Japan and the Philippines.

Figure 4 plots the long-term history of federal debt as a percentage of GDP over the last century.[15] As we can see, federal debt as a percentage of GDP was very low by today's standards before the Great Depression (below 20 percent). The ratio then more than doubled shortly after FDR took office and signed the New Deal. The debt level stayed around 40 percent of GDP through much of the 1930s and early 1940s, and then it quickly shot up to more than 100 percent of GDP after the United States entered World War II. After World War II, the debt level as a percentage of GDP underwent more than three decades of steady decline. This was uninterrupted by the Korean War and the Vietnam War. This decline ended in 1982, after President Reagan took office. Since then, except for a brief period in the late 1990s during the dot-com bubble, the debt level percentage has ascended steadily. The pace of ascent quickened greatly after President Obama took office in 2009. This was largely due to the financial crisis of 2008. By 2015, the federal debt level had reached 100 percent of GDP, rivaling the peak level last reached at the end of World War II.

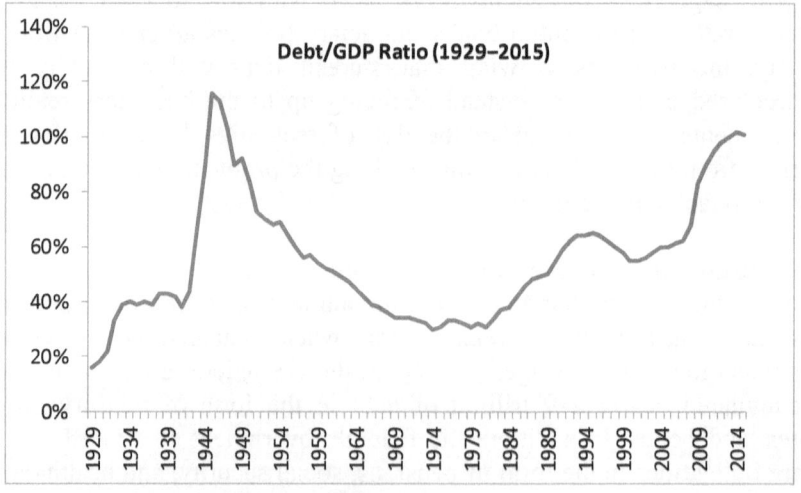

Figure 4 Debt/GDP Ratio (1929–2015)
Data Source: Kimberly Amadeo, www.thebalance.com

---

[15] I would like to thank Kimberly Amadeo for granting me the permission to use the data referenced in footnote 14 for this figure.

A Closer Look at the Federal Debt during and after World War II

As one can imagine, the federal debt and deficit during the World War II period were dominated by wartime spending. As illustrated in table 1, the amount of defense spending increased nearly fiftyfold, from $1.66 billion in 1940 to $82.97 billion in 1945. Its percentage within the total government outlay increased from 17.5 percent in 1940 to an astonishing 89.5 percent in 1945. Furthermore, by the time the war ended in 1945, military spending was 37.5 percent of GDP.

Table 1   Defense Spending during World War II

Year	1940	1941	1942	1943	1944	1945	1946
Defense Spending (in million $)	1,660	6,435	25,658	66,699	79,143	82,965	42,681
Defense as a % of Total Outlay	17.5%	47.1%	73.0%	84.9%	86.7%	89.5%	77.3%
Defense as a % of GDP	1.7%	5.6%	17.8%	37.0%	37.8%	37.5%	19.2%

Data source: Office of Management and Budget

The fact that federal debt during that time was nearly entirely due to defense spending made it relatively easy for the federal government to deleverage. After the war ended, military spending subsided quickly. By 1950, defense spending had dropped to only $13.7 billion, representing 32.2 percent of total government outlay.[16] Nevertheless, the federal government continued to run budget deficits for most of the postwar years, as is illustrated in figure 5.[17]

That the debt-to-GDP ratio steadily declined (figure 4) even while the federal government continued to run deficits in most years between 1946 and 1982 is the mathematical consequence of the economy growing faster than debt during that period. Therefore, it's fair to say that in the postwar period, America solved its debt problem largely by growing the economy rather than by austerity. Still, American taxpayers made their financial sacrifices. The tax rate for the bottom bracket went from 4.4 percent in 1940 to 23 percent in 1945 and stayed elevated throughout the 1950s and 1960s. The tax rate for the top bracket, which was dramatically raised in 1932 from 25 percent to 63 percent as a result of the New Deal, went up further during the war and reached 94 percent by

---

[16] "Historical Tables: Budget of the US Government," Office of Management and Budget, table 3.1, 2017, https://www.whitehouse.gov/sites/default/files/omb/budget/fy2017/assets/hist.pdf.

[17] "Historical Tables," tables 3.1 and 10.1.

1945. The top rate stayed above 90 percent until 1964, and then it was lowered to 77 percent—still a high rate by today's standards. The top tax rate remained above 69 percent until it was further lowered to 50 percent in 1982, after President Reagan took office.[18]

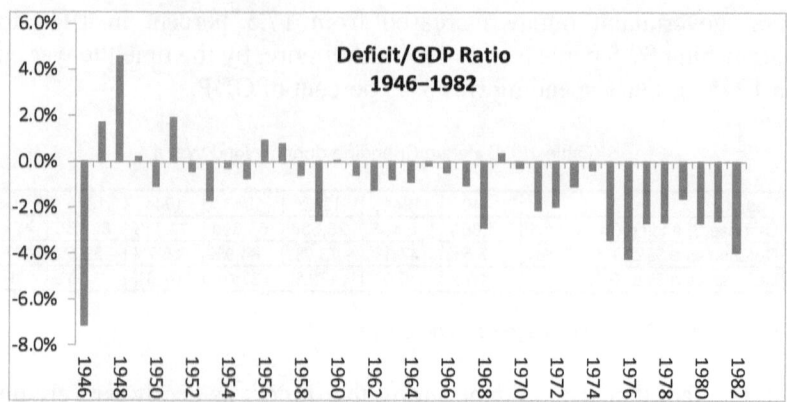

Figure 5 Deficit/GDP Ratio 1946–1982
Data Source: Office of Management and Budget

The Federal Deficit Today

The federal deficit situation today is very different from the World War II period. As seen in table 2,[19] defense no longer dominates the total outlay today. Instead, mandatory spending, which I define as health, Medicare, income security, and social security, has consistently exceeded 50 percent of the total outlay since the 1990s, and it is getting even bigger as time goes on.

Because any cut in mandatory spending would inevitably face voter resistance, resulting in automatic political suicide for any politician who proposed it, it is unsurprising that both political parties allowed the mandatory spending to grow unchecked. This resulted in an increasingly worsening financial situation for the federal government. While this was going on at the federal level, similar dynamics were also taking place at the state and municipal levels. As a result, many states and cities are saddled with heavy financial burdens in the form of public-sector employee union pension obligations. Some are even near insolvency.

---

[18] For a history of tax rates, visit TaxFoundation.org.

[19] "Historical Tables," tables 1.1, 3.1, and 10.1.

Table 2 Defense and Mandatory Spending, 1988–2015

		Reagan	Bush (I)	Clinton	Bush (II)	Obama
Fiscal Year		1988	1992	2000	2008	2015
Defense Spending	US Dollars (in Bilions)	290	298	294	616	590
	% of Total Outlay	27.3%	21.6%	16.5%	20.7%	16.0%
	% of GDP	5.6%	4.6%	2.9%	4.2%	3.3%
Madatory Spending	US Dollars (in Bilions)	473	696	1,015	1,720	2,425
	% of Total Outlay	44.4%	50.4%	56.7%	57.7%	65.7%
	% of GDP	9.2%	10.8%	10.0%	11.7%	13.6%
Surplus (Deficit)	US Dollars (in Bilions)	(155)	(290)	236	(459)	(438)
	% of GDP	-3.0%	-4.5%	2.3%	-3.1%	-2.5%

Data Source: Office of Management and Budget

Tax Disparity between Corporations and Individuals

The central question in tackling the debt problem lies in finding a ratio between tax revenue increases and spending reductions. Such a ratio can only be achieved if the majority of citizens perceive it to be fair. Given the dominant nature of the mandatory spending within the federal government's budget, any proposal that does not seriously reform these mandatory spending programs is most likely impractical over the long run.

Regarding tax revenues, it's evident that significant structural changes have taken place over the last one hundred years, as illustrated in figure 6.[20] In the prewar period, the biggest component of federal receipts was excise taxes, and individual tax and corporate tax contributed less than 20 percent each. Both the individual tax and the corporate tax were raised substantially during World War II, with corporate tax contributing about 40 percent and individual tax contributing about 45 percent during the war period. In the postwar period, however, individual tax remained remarkably steady at roughly 45 percent of the total federal receipts, but corporate tax enjoyed a steady decline, stabilizing at around 10 percent since the 1980s.

The striking disparity between individual tax and corporate tax was discussed in a separate detailed Government Accountability Office

---

[20] "Historical Tables," table 2.1.

study.[21] That study found that effective tax rates for corporations could be very different from statutory tax rates. Indeed, the effective corporate tax rate in the United States has declined steadily, from around 40 percent near the end of World War II to below 20 percent currently.[22] It is no doubt that this disparity is largely a result of persistent corporate lobbying over several decades. In a democracy, voices always sound louder and more effective if they are organized. Today, virtually all large corporations and industry groups have their own political action committees and their political donations and lobbying efforts over the years have enabled them to reduce their tax obligations (on a relative basis). Individual taxpayers, being unorganized and poorly financed, are left to foot much of the bill.

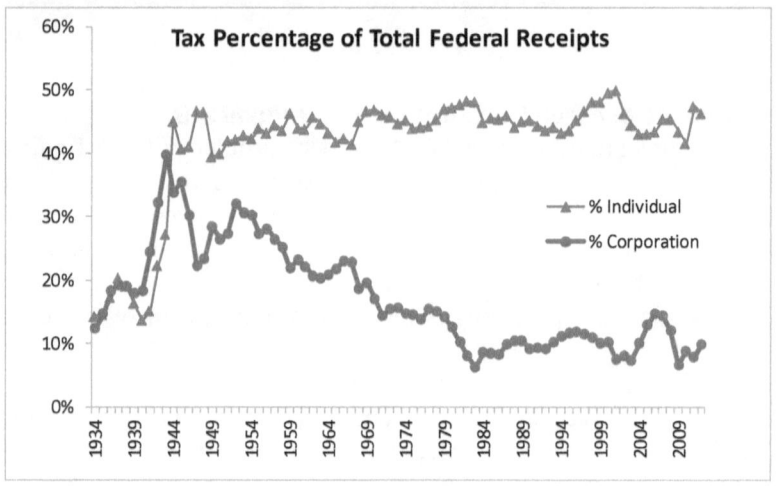

Figure 6 Tax Percentage of Total Federal Receipts
Data Source: Office of Management and Budget

Based on these discussions, it would seem that one easy way to increase tax revenue would be to increase the corporate taxes. In practice, though, that would prove difficult. Today, the United States has

---

[21] "Corporate Income Tax: Effective Tax Rates Can Differ Significantly from the Statutory Rate," United States Government Accountability Office, May 2013, http://www.gao.gov/assets/660/654957.pdf.

[22] "US Effective Corporate Tax Rate 1947–2011," Wikipedia, September 25, 2012, http://en.wikipedia.org/wiki/File:US_Effective_Corporate_Tax_Rate_1947-2011_v2.jpg.

one of the highest corporate tax rates in the world, and US corporations remain competitive largely by being extremely efficient and taking advantage of various tax loopholes. Eliminating these tax loopholes without significantly reducing the corporate tax rate would eventually drive many companies out of the country. In 2014, tax inversion tactics, in which US companies merge with foreign companies and move their headquarters to lower-tax jurisdictions, became increasingly popular. These cross-border transactions serve as warnings to political leaders that further political gridlock and inaction will cause permanent damage to the competitiveness of our corporations.

A Crisis Waiting to Happen

It is clear from the preceding discussions that, because of the dominant levels of mandatory spending in government outlays and the difficulty in restraining the mandatory spending, we cannot hope to solve our financial difficulties without first carrying out political reforms.

Recent efforts to reduce the deficit and slow the growth of national debt have not provided much comfort. A debt ceiling showdown in 2011 caused the stock market to tumble nearly 20 percent in a short time, and a last-minute decision to delay the problem and avoid a default pushed the debt ceiling to 2013. The debt ceiling crisis in 2013 caused the federal government to be partially shut down for more than two weeks. Unable to reach an agreement, the debt ceiling was once again postponed until early 2014. Following the debt ceiling crisis in the fall of 2013, both parties seemed to have learned their lessons—albeit the wrong lessons. While Republicans learned the hard way that using the debt ceiling as leverage is a losing tactic, Democrats learned that not negotiating on the debt ceiling is a winning strategy. Therefore, in February 2014, the debt ceiling was quickly postponed once again until March 2015. This was done without much debate or drama.

The debt ceiling crisis in 2011 and 2013 caused the United States to lose its AAA credit rating with the rating agency Standard and Poor's. Furthermore, it created chaos, and it revealed our government's inability to make tough choices. This greatly damaged what was once the impeccable image of America in the international community. It also greatly poisoned the atmosphere of our national politics. As a result, America became more polarized.

The failure to reach a reasonable deal during 2011 and 2013 meant America lost an opportunity to proactively solve its debt problem. In hindsight, this is not totally surprising. With the bond market still so accommodating (partly aided by the Federal Reserve's quantitative easing programs) and government bonds still being viewed as safe havens every time a crisis occurs in other parts of the world, politicians naturally felt no urgency to tackle the debt problem, which would have put their political careers at risk. Since 2013, there has been a sense of debt fatigue among the people and the politicians, and national debt is no longer on the forefront of our national dialogue. The issue of national debt was not even much discussed and debated during the presidential election in 2016. However, as deficit is poised to worsen rapidly beyond 2018, due to the flood of retiring baby boomers, continued failure to deal with the debt problem in a timely fashion means there will eventually be a crisis of confidence in the bond market, and it will be up to the capital markets to impose discipline on government finances. Should that happen, it would be extremely painful for investors as well as for citizens.

EPILOGUE

The Era of Turbulence and Polarization

As I wrap up this little book at the tail end of the unusual 2016 presidential election, I grow more and more convinced that we are living in turbulent times that will become even more tumultuous in the coming years and decades. The adoption of socialism while abandoning capitalism and the increasingly bitter polarization within society were symptoms that were widely on display throughout the 2016 presidential election campaign. They are the harbingers of more political challenges and social stresses to come. Aided by increasing trade and globalization and facilitated by advances in technology, the world is changing, and the pace of change is getting exponentially more rapid. Consequently, we see disruptions and dislocations in many aspects of our daily lives.

In Western Europe, after decades of socialism and debt-financed social-welfare programs, many of these countries have accumulated enormous amounts of debt, and their governments can no longer rely on the bond market to continue financing their social-welfare programs. In addition, the recent massive inflow of refugees and immigrants has disrupted the lives of many people, creating widespread resentment and division. The immediate result was the United Kingdom's exit from the European Union and more political instability in many other countries.

In the United States, where American people have traditionally embraced capitalism, more and more people, especially young millennials, now favor socialism, as was recently witnessed by the surprisingly strong popularity of the socialist presidential candidate Bernie Sanders. Polarization is increasing and becoming disturbingly more toxic, as demonstrated by the following events:

- Lois Lerner, a former IRS official, was accused of using her position to target conservative organizations, denying them due process and protected rights—an act bordering on political persecution.
- Supreme Court Justice Ruth Bader Ginsburg risked politicizing the high court by calling Donald Trump a "faker," and she said she would "move to New Zealand" if Donald Trump were elected president.
- The unexpected death of conservative justice Antonin Scalia in 2016 tipped the balance within the Supreme Court, and Republican senators blocked the nomination of Judge Merrick Garland, citing the upcoming presidential election.
- The 2016 election campaign has been the most unusual and

divisive in recent history. Given the extreme negatives for both candidates, it is clear that Americans are resorting more to extreme political populism than objective and conscientious judgment.

- Political polarization spread to traditionally silent and neutral US military leaders. Retired US Army Lieutenant General Michael Flynn spoke at the Republican National Convention, while retired US Marine General John Allen spoke at the Democratic National Convention. This prompted another retired general, Martin Dempsey, to pen a letter to the *Washington Post* on July 30, 2016, arguing that "military leaders do not belong at political conventions."[23]
- Nowhere is political polarization more prominent than in American news media. As Howard Marks, the chairman of Oaktree Capital Group, observed, the news media acts more like campaign spokespeople than objective news organizations.[24]

Is Socialism Destined to Be Our Future?

Throughout history, we have witnessed overwhelming evidence that socialism eventually leads to political oppression and social failure, while capitalism has been responsible for much of the prosperity the Western world has enjoyed. Today, however, people's fascination with and attraction to socialism has never been stronger in the Western democratic countries. The sovereign debt crisis in Europe has done little to shake Europeans' socialistic beliefs, and younger Americans, believing capitalism is responsible for all the ills of society, ranging from the financial crisis to their own student debts, are embracing socialism with increasing fervor.

Such is the nature of human societies. While our founders bestowed upon us the US Constitution, which allowed every able man and woman to pursue liberty and happiness to their maximum potential, they failed to

---

[23] "Military Leaders Do Not Belong at Political Conventions," Letter to the Editor, *The Washington Post*, July 30, 2016, https://www.washingtonpost.com/opinions/military-leaders-do-not-belong-at-political-conventions/2016/07/30/0e06fc16-568b-11e6-b652-315ae5d4d4dd_story.html.

[24] "August 2016 Memo," Howard Marks, Oaktree Capital Group, LLC, August 2016, https://www.oaktreecapital.com/.

foresee that with progress and prosperity would come inequality and poverty. Once inequality and poverty reach critical mass, socialism emerges as a way of wealth redistribution, and democracy becomes the tyranny of the majority. In that scenario, taxes will become increasingly progressive—until they are unbearably oppressive. Moral hazards will be increasingly rampant—until morals completely break down. Government debt will continue to pile up—until the market is no longer willing to participate in this government-sponsored Ponzi scheme. Are these things destined to be our future? Only time will tell.

ABOUT THE AUTHOR

Originally trained as a theoretical physicist, Dr. Weixiong Li has been working in the financial industry for more than twenty years. He currently manages a private investment partnership and lives with his wife, Cindy, in the suburbs of Chicago.

www.ingramcontent.com/pod-product-compliance
Lightning Source LLC
Chambersburg PA
CBHW030542290526
45786CB00004B/1827